CONTENTS

Left Brian Goodchild's classic picture of the mineral extension and gate just east of Abergynolwyn station was used as a frontispiece in Tom Rolt's *Railway Adventure*, in which he described the early years of the Talyllyn Railway Preservation Society (TRPS). Titled 'Road to Adventure', it epitomised the old TR with two wavering rails in the grass. This was typical of the track on the railway in 1951 and demonstrates the challenge faced by the TRPS.

In 1996 the gate-post on the left still stands, a gnarled relic supported on a metal stake, but nearly everything else has changed. The hills are covered in conifers, the rails are straight and to gauge, telephone lines run alongside the track, but the challenge of maintaining the TR still remains. *Brian Goodchild, TR Collection/DJM*

Below Tywyn Wharf: the notice board by the door advises that services will start on 4 June 1951. Signs of TRPS activity are the permanent way materials in the yard, and the sign and flag on the building. The challenge of restoring the TR has just started. The first 'amateur'-run train in the world had just run, on 14 May 1951, inaugurating the railway preservation movement. *Photo P. B. Bold*

Tal-y-llyn Railway

Whitsun 1951

The line will be re-opened for traffic between Towyn Wharf and Rhydyronen stations on **WHIT MONDAY ONLY, MAY 14th** Trains will leave Towyn Wharf station for Rhydyronen at the following times:-

10 a.m., 11-30 a.m., 2-30 p.m., 4 p.m.
(an additional evening train may run if required).

It is hoped to resume services throughout on June 1st, 1951 and a suitable announcement will shortly be made.

L. T. C. ROLT,
General Manager.

J. BASIL JONES & CO., Cambrian Press, Red Lion Street, Towyn.

The debate continues regarding the meaning of railway preservation. A line like the TR, which carried a few thousand passengers a year in pre-Society days, has to alter to carry the much larger numbers of tourists today, and their fares are essential to support the line. Although the layout has changed, a platform has been built, and the corner cut back to ease the curve, No 1 can still stand at Nant Gwernol with the same coach, as it did on a special working for the owner's family about 100 years ago. The public could not enjoy the Gwernol ravine until the extension opened on 22 May 1976. *TR Collection, courtesy W. McConnel/TE*

BRITISH RAILWAYS

PAST and PRESENT
Special

THE TALYLLYN RAILWAY

Tal-y-Llyn Railway

A

PUBLIC MEETING

will be held at

THE INSTITUTE, TOWYN,

on

TUESDAY, MARCH 27th, 1951

at 7-30 p.m.

The Committee of the Tal-y-llyn Railway Preservation Society will explain their proposals and cordially invite all who are interested in the future of the local line to attend and express their views.

THE TAL-Y-LLYN RAILWAY PRESERVATION SOCIETY

P. B. WHITEHOUSE,
Hon. Secretary.

J. BASIL JONES & CO., Cadvan Press, Red Lion Street, Towyn.

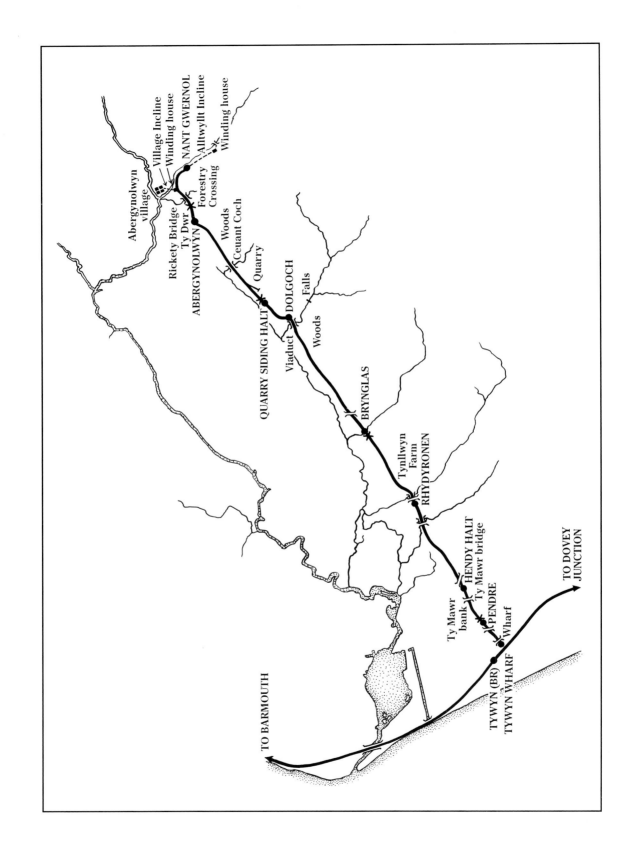

BRITISH RAILWAYS

PAST and PRESENT
Special

THE TALYLLYN RAILWAY

A nostalgic trip along the world's first preserved railway

David J. Mitchell
&
Terry Eyres

Issued 19 May 1959

Past and Present

Past & Present Publishing Ltd

First published in September 1996

British Library Cataloguing in Publication Data

A catalogue record for this book is available from the British Library.

ISBN 1 85895 125 9

Past & Present Publishing Ltd
Unit 5
Home Farm Close
Church Street
Wadenhoe
Peterborough PE8 5TE
Tel (01832) 720440
Fax (01832) 720531
e-mail: pete@slinkp-p.demon.co.uk

Map on page 2 drawn by Christina Siviter; other maps by C. K. Theobald.

Printed and bound in Great Britain

INTRODUCTION

The Talyllyn Railway has several claims to fame. The first narrow gauge railway in Britain to be built for steam operation, it survived, unaltered, for 85 years, little known and defying the norms of engineering, until it became the first railway in the world to be taken over and run by enthusiasts. It is one of the very few railways that still runs the trains that opened the line in regular service.

The railway is 7¼ miles long and runs from the coastal town of Tywyn, where it terminates alongside the Cambrian Coast line. The statutory railway ended at Abergynolwyn, 6½ miles from Tywyn, and passenger trains terminated there. The tracks continued as a mineral tramway for a further three-quarters of a mile to Nant Gwernol. Here the Alltwyllt incline lifted the tracks up to the three-quarter-mile-long horse-worked Galltymoelfre tramway leading to the Cantrybedd incline, which rose up to the bottom level of Bryn Eglwys Quarry.

The railway was built to enable the slate from the quarry to reach the sea, and both railway and quarry were developed by a group of Manchester businessmen seeking to diversify from their cotton businesses, then threatened by lack of raw material due to the American Civil War. The railway was simply the means of extracting the slate, and the opening of the standard gauge coastal railway in October 1863 meant that slate could be transhipped at Tywyn, and the planned continuation to Aberdovey Harbour was unnecessary.

The records are unclear, but it seems certain that the line was already under construction when the Act of Parliament was obtained on 5 July 1865, and the purpose of obtaining the Act is unclear (see the history by Boyd, listed in the Bibliography). The railway as built was laid with 44 lb wrought iron rails to a gauge of 2 ft 3 in. There were two locomotives, four four-wheeled carriages, a brake-van and some 115 wagons, mainly slate-carrying, but also ones for coal, closed vans, and gunpowder vans. This initial equipment was to last the TR until 1951.

The quarrying enterprise was not successful, and in October 1879 the quarry and railway were offered for sale by auction. They failed to sell, and in 1882 William McConnel, one of the original founders, bought both for £18,000, although £200,000 had been invested. McConnel ran the quarry with reasonable success, and was succeeded by his son in 1902. The strike at the great Penrhyn Quarry produced prosperity in the early 1900s, but the drop in slate prices following the end of the strike, and the fact that the quarry leases were due to expire in 1910, caused the quarry to close at the end of 1909. The stocks were cleared and the machinery at the quarry began to be dismantled.

Quarry and railway were saved when Mr H. Haydn Jones, MP for Meirionnydd, bought the undertaking in 1911. Sir Haydn, as he became, ran both quarry and railway, but no money was available for improvements, and it was very much 'make do and mend'. A roof fall caused the quarry to close in 1946, and thereafter the railway survived on the small local traffic, and some summer tourists. Sir Haydn, by then in his 80s, kept the railway running, although it cost him £5 a week to do so. That the original equipment kept going for 85 years is a tribute to the original builders and the dedicated staff at Tywyn who maintained them with little in the way of tools, and less money. After seeing No 1's firebox, Tom Rolt comments in *Railway Adventure* that it was a brave man who fired her on her last journey.

When Sir Haydn died in June 1950, the railway continued to run until the end of the season, but closure and scrapping seemed inevitable. However, a group of enthusiasts had met in Birmingham in October of that year to see if the TR could be saved. Following negotiations with Sir Haydn's executors, Lady Haydn generously handed over the TR to the newly formed Talyllyn Railway Preservation Society.

In the austere days after the Second World War, it was a novel and possibly foolhardy venture. The first volunteer-run trains ran on 14 May 1951, inaugurating the railway preservation movement. Increased traffic, necessary to fund the preservation of the TR, brought its own problems, and the two priorities were to have an engine to work the train and track to run it on. It was a close-run thing, and only by about 1954 did the TR reach a state where the outlook was secure. The story of the first two years is told in Tom Rolt's classic book.

The newly formed TRPS faced many problems. The only workable loco, *Dolgoch*, was 85 years old and still had its original boiler, although it had had an overhaul in 1948 when it cracked a frame. With the unusual gauge of 2 ft 3 in and a very restricted loading gauge, few locos were available to work on the TR. The neighbouring Corris Railway had the same gauge and an even tighter loading gauge, and although closed in 1948, two locos still lay at Machynlleth. These were bought and transferred to Tywyn, the first new rolling-stock in 85 years. No 3 was in working order, but due to the wheel treads being slightly narrow, and the TR track being about 1 inch over-gauge (due to No 1's rigid wheelbase) she would not stay on the track, and in 1951 No 2 ran the service unaided, and kept the TR alive. The Hunslet Engine Co kindly overhauled No 4 for the 1952 season, which eased the loco problem.

The increased traffic meant that the track was literally falling apart faster than the TRPS could replace the cracked rails and rotten sleepers. The Territorial Army exercise in 1953, when the TA relaid a couple of miles, was the turning point, and thereafter the track gradually improved.

Increased traffic also needed more coaches. Some open bodies were donated by the Penrhyn Railway, and the purchase of two mine car bogie chassis gave the TR its first bogie coaches. Further open coaches were built at Tywyn, and bodies of two Glyn Valley coaches

Keeping on track: an appeal inserted in the Committee Report on 31 January 1952, and the back page of the second issue of *Tal-y-llyn News*, of November 1953, showing the considerable voluntary activity, but appealing for still more funds.

TALYLLYN RAILWAY PRESERVATION SOCIETY

Do You Know!

THAT £1 WILL

BUY 3 SLEEPERS

BUY 12 PAIRS OF FISHPLATES

BUY 40 KEYS

BUY 4 Cwt. OF COAL

BUY 6 GALLONS OF OIL

BUY 1,000 TICKETS

MAINTAIN PERMANENT WAY FOR 3 HOURS

MEET COST OF RATES, INSURANCE, ELECTRICITY & WATER FOR 1 WEEK

PROVIDE MISCELLANEOUS STORES FOR 1 WEEK

A DONATION OF £8.0.0 will cover the cost of purchase and installation of a 24 foot length of single track, including ballasting. Why not buy a length or form a group to adopt a section of the line.

Remittances should be sent to the Honorary Treasurer at:- 36, Waterloo Street, Birmingham, 2.

16   SOCIETY DIARY

29 Nov- 5 Dec.Cardiff & Dist.Federation of Model Clubs & Societies. Exhibition at Sophia Gardens Pavilion, Cardiff. TRPS Stand. Members able to assist as stewards write to Mr.Harvey Gray, 233 West Boulevard, Birmingham, 32.
2 Dec. London Area Annual Meeting, 2nd Floor, Railway Clearing House, 203, Eversholt St., N.W.1, 6.30 for 6.45 pm. Photo & Film Show to follow.
8 Dec. Talk - Norwood M.R.C.
18-20 Dec. Manchester Model Railway Society Exhibition, Corn Exchange, Manchester. TRPS Stand.
5 Jan. 1954. N.W.Area New Year Social & Working Party, at Towyn.
6 Jan. Talk - Round Table, Acton.
20 Jan. Talk - London University College Railway Soc.
21 Jan. Talk - Stephenson Locomotive Society, Russell Road, London, W.14.
6 Feb. Norwood M.R.C. Exhibition. TRPS Stand.
9 Feb. Talk - Imperial College Railway Society (London)
10 Feb. N.W.Area Re-Union. (see Area Notes).

N.W.Area Working Parties 21st November, 1st January, 20th February, 20th March, 16th April (Easter).
Please notify Mr.Harvey Gray (address above) if you know of any Model Exhibitions or other suitable functions, so that T.R.P.S. publicity can be arranged.
===
FROM THE TREASURER Between now and 1st February, when subscriptions should come rolling in, considerable financial embarrassment is likely, as Army Re-laying Expenditure has exceeded Appeal Receipts by £400; may I appeal to members who have not contributed, or feel they can send more, to send me a donation as soon as possible.
To those who feel they cannot afford it may I say we quite understand, but perhaps you can ease the position by sending your 1954 subscription a little early. The payment of wages to our small and loyal Staff is entirely dependent on Members' response to this appeal, and I hope you will do your best to tide us over this difficult period. The address is: Patrick J.Garland, 36, Waterloo St., Birmingham, 2. Please rally round.

Printed and Published for the T.R.P.S. by R. W. Inkster, 2 Woodlands Lane, Altrincham, Cheshire. Tel. Alt. 0468

and one from the Corris were recovered and restored. But it was obvious that further coaches would be needed. No 18 was a six-compartment bogie coach, its styling based on the Glyn Valley coaches. These had straight sides, making construction easier than the tumblehome of the TR coaches. Built entirely at Tywyn, it is a masterpiece of craftsmanship. However, it was realised that the limited number of volunteers with the necessary skills would limit the pace at which new coaches could be built, and thereafter the bodies were built commercially by Tisdale and finished at Tywyn, where the chassis were built.

The growth in traffic led to the sectioning of the line, with loops at Pendre and Brynglas, and train staffs. In the peak season trains would pass at the latter place. By the 1960s arrangements were made for operation of three train sets with the building of a loop at Quarry Siding, and the upgrading of Pendre to allow passenger trains to pass. For the centenary year in 1965 Wharf was remodelled and became a proper station for the first time. Passengers demanded better facilities, and the slate shed at Abergynolwyn was inadequate. Refreshments had been sold from the little office there, and when this proved unsatisfactory, a mobile refreshment van was provided. In the winter of 1968/69 the site was cleared and a new building erected with suitable facilities for passengers and staff.

Beyond Abergynolwyn the mineral extension still remained much as it had been in Sir Haydn's time. The track beyond the Winding House had been lifted in 1952, but everything else remained as a reminder of how the line had been, and provided a pleasant walk through the oak woods overlooking the village of Abergynolwyn and going up the narrow Gwernol Valley to the site of the sidings at the foot of the Alltwyllt incline. The TRPS had always wanted to extend the passenger service along this section. However, it was not part of the statutory railway, being a mineral tramway built with wayleaves over the land. It took many years of patient work to ascertain ownership of the various parcels of land, and to acquire a Light Railway Order to enable reconstruction, which would involve easing curves and levelling out the gradients.

Construction started with a first blasting on 3 October 1970 and, following approval by the Railway Inspectorate, the extension was opened on 22 May 1976 by Mr Wynford Vaughan Thomas. The opening brought the TR to its present state. The stations at Abergynolwyn and Wharf have been extended, improved passenger facilities provided, a further carriage shed built, and many detailed improvements made.

A fifth steam engine had come in 1954, when No 6 was given to the TR by Abelson & Co, and regauged from 2 ft 0 in. The need for a more powerful steam engine was seen in the 1960s, when traffic was growing rapidly. A 3-foot-gauge loco was therefore bought and rebuilt over the years, entering service in 1991 as No 7, named after Tom Rolt, one of the founders of the TR. Today three diesel engines are in use on engineering trains.

A major development being carried out is the fitting of continuous brakes, a requirement for passenger trains since the 1889 Regulation of Railways Act. Mr McConnel had argued against its application to the TR on the grounds of cost, and the low speed of the trains, and gained exemption. The TR has worked safely ever since, but the heavier trains and freer-running stock with roller bearings put a strain on the loco brakes, and air-brakes are being fitted to most coaches, worked by air-pumps on the locos.

The rapid growth of traffic seen in the 1960s did not continue, and economic problems and increased competition from other railways and other tourist attractions has meant that the TR has had to fight to maintain revenue and traffic. Preservation of the railway as it was in 1950 would have been impossible, but the line remains as an example of a Victorian narrow gauge railway. Gleaming locos, burning coal, haul trains of wooden-bodied coaches up the valley of the Fathew, under the shadow of Cader Idris. The TR provides pleasure both for the visitors who come to ride, and for the many members of the TRPS who come to work on all aspects of the line. All trains are operated, and much of the maintenance carried out, by volunteers, while a small skilled staff provides expertise, particularly in the engineering department. The TRPS remains a friendly line for both visitors and volunteers, and as it approaches its Golden Jubilee, it still sets an example of the best in railway preservation.

The TR did not change greatly in the first 85 years, and many of the pictures of that era have already been published. For many of the 'past' pictures, therefore, we have drawn on early TRPS views, depicting a period when change was occurring and also showing the activities of early railway preservation. There are few pre-1960s pictures of TR trains in the countryside, and the scenes themselves have not changed greatly, so the majority of the views are around the stations. With a self-contained railway like the TR, it is also possible to observe the changes in the stock over the years, and in addition to views along the line we have included pictures of locos and coaches.

Welsh place-name spelling has been much altered in recent years. The TR has not been particularly affected, but we have used current spelling throughout: Tywyn for Towyn, and Meirionnydd for Merioneth.

ACKNOWLEDGEMENTS

This book has been prepared on behalf of the Talyllyn Railway Preservation Society. Nigel Adams introduced the idea, which was supported by the Council of the TRPS. Many members and friends of the TR have helped, providing photographs, memorabilia, advice and information, identifying locations and facilitating the taking of the 'present' pictures. These include Derek Allen, John Bate, Llew Bedder, Eric Bruton, Eddie Castellan, J. J. Davis, John Halliday, Michael Howard, Harry Koster, Steve Powell, John Slater and Keith Walton. Richard Casserley kindly made his father's and his own pictures available. The Historical Model Railway Society (HMRS) printed J. J. Davis's negatives. Many members of the Talyllyn Railway staff and TRPS helped in taking the 'present' shots by moving stock, posing trains and enabling replica views to be taken.

Thanks are also due to the many photographers, both known and unknown, who have provided pictures for the TR archives over the years; they have been credited where they are known. Terry Eyres has taken many of the 'present' views and has printed other negatives. Sue Whitehouse proof-read the text.

To all those who have helped in any way, my thanks; the responsibility for picture selection and accuracy is mine alone.

David J. Mitchell

BIBLIOGRAPHY

Boyd, J. I. C. *The Talyllyn Railway* (Wild Swan)
Holmes, A. T. *Slates from Abergynolwyn* (Gwynedd Archives; reprint planned)
Rolt, L. T. C. *Railway Adventure* (Constable 1953, latest reprint Alan Sutton)
White, A. C. *40 years of the TR* (A. B. Publishing)
Talyllyn Railway *Talyllyn Handbook*
Talyllyn Railway *Talyllyn Guide*

Boyd is the definitive history of the TR up to 1950, while Rolt is the story of the first years of the TRPS. All books are available from the Talyllyn Railway Shop, Wharf Station, Tywyn, Gwynedd LL36 9EY (Tel 01654 711012).

Tywyn Wharf

Most of the slate carried on the TR was transhipped on to the main line at Tywyn Wharf. Opened on 24 October 1863 by the Aberystwyth & Welsh Coast Railway, the Cambrian Coast line was successively operated by the Cambrian Railways, Great Western Railway and BR. When Eric Bruton came to Tywyn on the first TR AGM special (ex-GWR Railcar No W13) on 26 September 1953, he ended his day photographing Collett 0-6-0 No 3202 entering Tywyn on the evening Machynlleth-Pwllheli train. The Wharf siding and its loop can be seen to the left of the train, with the TR track on the top of the wharf.

Trees now obscure the exact location, so the 'present' view is more head-on. The Wharf siding has gone, although the centre line remains as an engineering siding. The TR yard is more cluttered, but the wharf-edge track remains. The signal has gone and only an illuminated indicator warns the driver that he is approaching the loop, now with sprung points as Tywyn signal box is closed and the line controlled by radio from Machynlleth. A Class 156 heads south on 30 May 1996; no locos now work the Coast Line, and the TR's coal comes by road. *E. D. Bruton/TE*

Before photographing No 3202, Eric Bruton took this charming shot of the last train of the day arriving at Wharf station at 5.42 pm. Loco No 4 is hauling van 5, a Brown Marshall coach, the Lancaster coach (No 4), and a roofed ex-Penrhyn coach. Two more Penrhyn bodies are on their sides and a slate wagon and two iron-bodied wagons stand on the siding. The track on the wharf edge is visible, as are the two wagon turntables that gave access to it. Some of the coal lumps look very large, and stocks appear high for the end of the season. The Tywyn down home is firmly on.

In 1996 the Narrow Gauge Railway Museum has been built on the site of the walled coal yard. The platform

has been angled northwards, and the headshunt extended to the wharf edge, causing the north end of the siding there to be removed. A Portacabin serves as a cafe, and the sectional garage is being refurbished to serve as a catering store. No 3 stands on the loco road, about to take coal and water. The TR has plans to rebuild Wharf station building, subject to funds being available. *E. D. Bruton/TE*

12

Toy Railway, Towyn

52538

Looking down the station approach in about 1900 we see No 2 waiting with a short train. The gunpowder store beyond is newly built, replacing a wooden structure; the dovecote is a novel feature. There is what looks like a gradient post near the bridge, but it may be an addition; early postcards are very unreliable as they were often altered to suit the publisher's ideas of what should be in the view. The house featured in later views, 'Trefri', has not been built.

In 1996 only the gunpowder shed serves to locate the shot. The toilet block hides the road bridge, widened in the 1950s, and the station extensions narrow the entrance, which is now gated, passengers being routed via the booking office and shop. The boulder is reputed to have come from Bryn Eglwys Quarry many years ago in response to a local lady asking Sir Haydn Jones for some rockery stone. No 1 waits with a photographic special.
Commercial postcard, D. Allen Collection/DJM

Top and middle Ken Cope sells tickets to what is either a school party or a very large family in about 1952. The office served as booking office, traffic office and railway headquarters. It had long been the sanctum of Edward Thomas, who served the TR from 1897 to 1950, for many years running the railway almost single-handed and continuing as a Director after the Society took over.

The former office and the adjacent store room have now been knocked into one room and serve as the Railway Shop; the door links the two scenes. *TR Collection/ DJM*

Bottom The current booking office is outside the door, where the building has been extended eastwards. This is the view from the door in the earlier picture. *E. Castellan*

Opposite page Looking north along the wharf edge in the 1960s, there was only a single track, with the curve round into the station. Penrhyn coach No 8 is being scrapped. The water tank has not been built, the Museum extension is under construction, and *Cambrai* stands outside. Built by Corpet et Louvet for the metre-gauge Chemin de Fer du Cambresis in northern France, *Cambrai* is part of the Museum's collection.

As already mentioned, the BR signal has been replaced by a point indicator. A second wharf siding has been laid on the right, and a reverse siding leads down to the ballast loading dock, where crushed stone ballast is tipped from road trucks on to a decking with trap-doors to gravity load TR ballast wagons. *Both DJM*

No 2 *Dolgoch* stands near the wharf edge on 25 August 1948. The quarry has closed, so the wagons are probably out of use; the one on the right is an incline wagon, designed to avoid spillage on the cable inclines. The BR line is in the background; the wagon of large rocks will be for the sea defences where the line runs along the seashore north of Tywyn.

No 3 poses on the headshunt in March 1996. The track on which No 2 stood was where the platform now is, and the track now extends to the wharf edge. *H. C. Casserley, courtesy R. M. Casserley/TE*

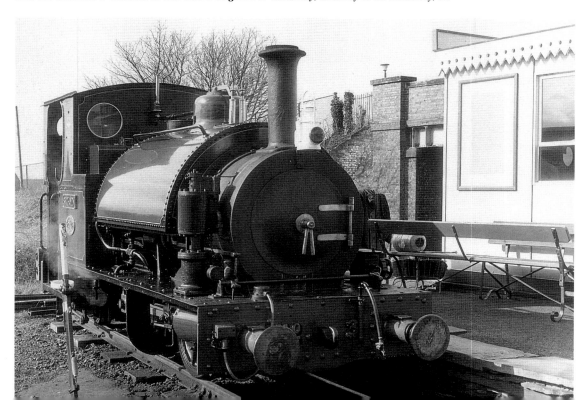

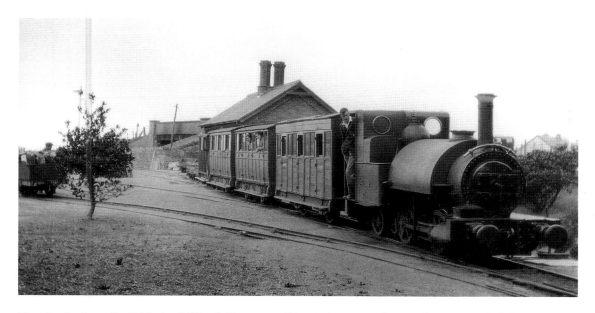

The classic view of a TR train at Wharf. The scene did not change much over the years and dating can often only be done by looking at details. Here No 1 heads a summer train of three coaches, the van and some empty wagons in 1933; the van still has a lookout on the south, non-platform, side. The photographer, Mr Riding, has his picture taken on the footplate. The chaired track is clearly visible and the wagon on the extreme left looks to be full of coal.

By 1996 the view has changed a great deal, with the Wharf building extensions and the toilet block obscuring the view of the road and the houses beyond; the roof of the original station building provides a reference. The first coach in the siding is No 4, the leading coach in the 1933 picture. No 3 is departing with the 12.30 train. *E. J. Riding/TE*

The view from the Aberdovey Road bridge gives a view of the station site. There seem to be few pre-1951 views from the bridge, and this wartime view (*above left*) dated September 1940 shows a deserted Wharf yard. Rows of slate await buyers, though Hitler's activities would soon increase demand, even for those sizes that were normally difficult to sell. The seat outside the office was the only passenger facility.

On 24 March 1957 (*left*) No 1 waits to be loaded on to a low-loader for transportation to the Midlands and overhaul. No 5, a TR coach and No 6 stand at the platform, while the cab on the left is part of *Russell*, the Welsh Highland 2-6-2T that spent a period of time at Tywyn, before eventually being restored and returned to Porthmadog. The layout now includes a run-round loop, and only the siding on the right remains of the original layout; the weighbridge remains, but is disconnected. Caravans have appeared in the fields near the sea.

The layout was completely remodelled in the winter of 1964/65 to create a proper station. The station building has been extended, and the chimneys shortened; with the removal of the chimney breast inside, they are dummies. The Cafe and Museum are behind the awning, and housing has appeared beyond the BR line. The siding on the right leads to the wharf edge and the small engineers' yard, as No 2 leaves with the 11.20 train on 16 August 1993. *J. W. Sparrowe/J. C. W. Halliday/TE*

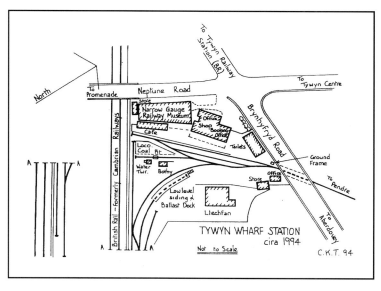

Map of Tywyn Wharf station, circa 1994. *C. K. Theobald*

19

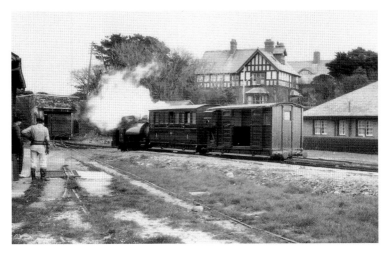

Top and middle Ex-Corris Railway No 3 stands on a short train at Wharf platform. The platform and loop have been relaid, but the near siding crossing the disconnected weighbridge is still in original TR condition. Edward Thomas lived in the black and white house overlooking the station.

Today the platform occupies the site of the sidings, and the layout has been slewed north, so the angle between building and platform is reduced. The centre siding is approximately on the alignment where No 3 stood, while No 1 stands on the loop with a photographic special organised by Push Pull Promotions to replicate a 1940s train, with a dirty loco, nameplates removed and the name painted on the tank. *R. K. Walton/DJM*

Bottom A view of No 1 waiting with a train in the late 1930s, taken from the other side of the station. All four coaches are present, the second being the Lancaster Carriage vehicle; worn wheels caused it to be known as 'Limping Lulu' in early Society days. *H. B. Tours, DJM collection*

Opposite page The line from Wharf to Pendre runs in a cutting round the south side of Tywyn. In 1967 No 6 coasts down the bank into Wharf station with the last train of the day.

During the winter of 1978/79 the cutting was deepened to ease the gradient facing departing trains, which involved steepening the cutting sides. On 24 March 1996 No 3 drifts down the deepened cutting with the stock for the 11.40 service. The cutting is now much more tree-grown. *Both DJM*

Pendre to Hendy

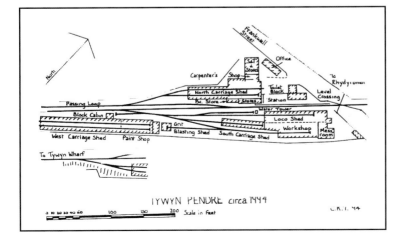

Top and middle Pendre is the operating and technical centre of the Talyllyn Railway. The group of buildings to the south of the line was built shortly after the opening of the line, and comprised a loco shed, a carriage shed, and a cottage for Mr Bousted, the fitter from Fletcher Jennings who came to Tywyn to supervise the loco department. The wooden carriage shed is believed to be a later extension, when the original carriage shed was turned into a workshop. In 1948 not much has changed since the 1870s.

By 1996 the original complex is much the same, but on the left-hand side the North carriage shed is just visible, and at the west end of the site the embankment has been dug out and a further carriage shed built, with a block post attached to control the points and house the token instruments. *H. C. Casserley, courtesy R. M. Casserley/TE*

Bottom Map of Pendre station circa 1994. *C. K. Theobald*

Opposite page Originally situated on the edge of the town, Pendre has gradually been surrounded by houses. In 1968 the Giesl ejector-fitted No 4 drifts through the yard. On the left is the rebuilt old carriage shed, while on the right is the North carriage shed, built on the site of a barn. The group of point levers at the rear of the train controls the west-end points, the east end loop points being locally controlled.

In 1996 the bank and green-house on the left have been removed and the West carriage shed and block post built on the site. The east loop points are now on the frame, although the points in the yard are still on local levers; the siding point has been relaid with a greater radius. No 3 passes with a set of air-braked stock. *DJM/TE*

No 3, working bunker first uphill through School Bridge, enters Pendre yard on 9 August 1957 with an 'express' train from Tywyn; the loco has been fitted with a form of spark-arrester. The padlock fastening the yard points is visible in the bottom left-hand corner.

Today the yard points are some 20 feet to the east, the loop has been lengthened and the bank dug out for the West carriage shed. The block post houses the lever frame and the token instruments, with rodding and point locks replacing the hand levers. The driver of No 3 on the up 'Quarryman' is about to exchange the single-line tokens with the blockman. *J. J. Davis, courtesy HMRS/DJM*

PENDRE GROUND FRAME

During 1958 the newly restored No 1 stands on the shed road, with Peter Bold, probably acting as fireman, posing by the cab. Peter served the TR for many years as Society Chairman and a Director of the Company. The North carriage shed steelwork is going up in the background, and the decayed South shed is just visible on the right.

No 1 is standing in the same spot in the 'present' shot. The carriage shed has been clad and lengthened, and the South shed rebuilt; the station building is just visible to the left of the latter. The frame alongside the loco is for drilling sleepers. *P. B. Bold/DJM*

This page In about 1910 No 2, then called *Pretoria*, passes through Pendre with a mixed train. The van still has doors and lookout on the south, non-platform, side. A gunpowder van stands on the siding, securely padlocked. The gentleman on the right could be Mr T. R. Perkins, a well-known writer on railways, whose brother took the photograph.

By August 1953 the trees have almost obliterated the bridge and house in the background. The loop and siding are still of original TR materials, but the main line has been relaid and the alignment of the shed road altered. No 2 receives attention between trains, standing at the head of a mixed rake of wagons and the ex-Corris van.

In 1996 No 1 stands on the main line, with the bridge parapet just visible at the rear. Carriage sheds have been built on both sides of the line and the block post is directly ahead. The wagon body on the ground is the former Corris mail wagon, waiting to be mounted on a new chassis as part of the museum fleet. *G. M. Perkins, DJM collection/R. K. Walton/DJM*

Opposite page No 1 moves out of the shed past the wooden South carriage shed in about 1930. Note the very large lumps of coal in the wagon. The rail to the right of the engine has suffered a collapsed web, a common failure of the wrought iron rails.

In 1996 the carriage shed has been rebuilt with a steel frame and a brick base. The shed smoke hood has been replaced by steel vents, and the east-end loop points are now controlled from the block post. The water tank was errected in 1952 to replace the earlier tank inside the shed. The coal wagon is one of the ex-Corris Railway vehicles known as 'Queen Marys'. *TRPS Collection/TE*

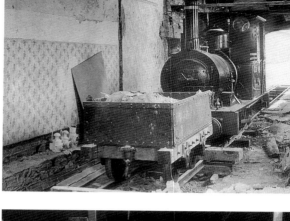

Pendre shed originally held two locomotives, and the east end wall divided it from the cottage. In the 1960s the increased services required three or four locos in steam daily, and the shed was lengthened by knocking through into the cottage, as seen *above*. During this work No 2 stands under the smoke hood. The boards on the left-hand wall give the firemen's and cleaners' duties, while the electrical trunking, formerly fastened to the east wall, is temporarily suspended from the roof beams.

Later (*above right*) No 2 stands on the temporary track extended into the erstwhile cottage. The wagon is being loaded with rubble from the internal walls.

Today (*right*) the rails extend through into the former cottage and the trunking is properly suspended. The duty boards have been moved to a position behind the photographer, and a stove now provides warmth in the winter. No 4, fitted with an air-pump, stands over the pit. *DJM (2)/TE*

Opposite page It is 1951 and the newly arrived Corris locos stand in Pendre Works. No 3 has had its tank and cab removed and is having a hydraulic boiler test; it has yet to be turned to face downhill. Above No 4 can be glimpsed the line shaft and pulley driven by a small engine that powered the primitive machines. Note that there is no electric light.

Today the works have power and newer machine-tools. There is also a steel frame with chain-blocks for lifting; formerly this was done from the roof beams. Creature comforts include a stove and a bench for tea-breaks. Pendre does all TR engineering work, except major boiler repairs, and is responsible for keeping the vintage engines and rolling-stock working. No 7 stands over the pit in the works where it was built. *P. B. Bold/TE*

No 1 heads a train into the platform in the 1930s. The rendered section of the building on the left is the cottage, with the loco shed beyond. On the right is the barn, and a passenger looks out from the wooden station building.

In 1996 the rendering has been removed from the building, and the wood/slate smoke ventilator replaced by more utilitarian metal stacks. The barn has gone, replaced by the North carriage shed, and the stores annex is visible behind the wall. The wooden station building is a replacement, and has acquired a modern litter-bin. *TR Collection/TE*

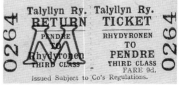

Issued 22 September 1967.

30

No 2 runs over Pendre level crossing with a down train on a wet Easter Saturday in 1965. The path giving access to the cottage is to the right of the engine.

In 1996 the crossing has been widened, but the lamp remains. The path has gone, and the cottage garden is now used for cutting firewood and storing point rodding. The slate plaque commemorates Herbert Jones, Locomotive Superintendent, who lived in the cottage for many years during TRPS days. No 3 is entering with a train of air-braked stock. *Both DJM*

The road that crosses the line east of Pendre station was originally a track leading to several farms. Traffic has increased over the years, particularly since a housing estate was built south of the line in the 1960s. The crossing was only one car's width, with a pair of metal gates, which had once been four separate gates, but which the TRPS modified by joining them in pairs; this probably made operating the gates easier. The crossing was widened in 1984 and new gates provided, complete with warning lights. In this March 1954 view No 4 stands on the crossing, while various TRPS members' cars are parked on the right. Although described as a morning scene, it is more likely an evening engineering train. *R. K. Walton*

In August 1954 No 3, then working bunker first to Abergynolwyn, leaves Pendre over the level crossing and up the grass-grown track. On the left is the shed/works/cottage building.

In 1996 it can be seen how the crossing has been widened and the hedge replaced by a white fence. On the left is the diesel storage tank. *J. J. Davis, courtesy HMRS/DJM*

No 2 heads up the track east of Pendre in the 1930s. No sleepers are visible, and the track between the rails suggests that the line was well used as a footpath.

Today the track is in good order. Old sleepers are stacked at the side, eventually to be cut up for firewood to light up the engines. *H. B. Tours, DJM collection/DJM*

The hollow area to the south of Ty Mawr embankment has been used for tipping loco ash, etc. Seen here is No 5, driven by TRPS Treasurer Colin Roobottom, pushing a pair of loaded tippers over the 'sliding siding', a temporary line laid on the already tipped material. It was connected to the main line by a curved section of rails that was slid over the running lines, with a ramp that carried the wagons off the main track. The flat wagons are the 'runners' used to push the tippers up the ramp, as the loco is too heavy for the temporary trackwork. *Both DJM*

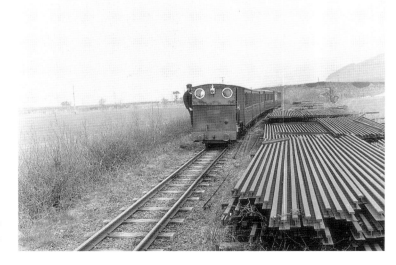

Today the filled area is used for storing rails. No 4 passes on a down train. *DJM*

In 1951 No 2 plods up the overgrown track with the three Brown Marshall coaches. The rails are just visible, and the track between the rails again suggests that the line was regularly used as a footpath.

Thirty years later No 3 heads a train of rails to Tywyn. The gang has been collecting used rails left in the cess after relaying. The last wagon came from Bowaters and is known as a 'Boflat'; it carries a small crane for lifting rails on board. The gang enjoys the evening sunshine while riding alfresco.

The re-roofing of Rhydyronen station in 1995 provided an excuse to run a slate train. The slate, however, came up the line from Tywyn, rather than down. Safely precludes running unbraked vehicles at the back of the train, so the slate wagons were marshalled ahead of the coaches. The train ran to Brynglas so the slate did in fact arrive at Rhydyronen from the correct direction. The industrial development is obvious in the background, and the railstacks in the previous picture can again be seen. *P. B. Bold collection/DJM/TE*

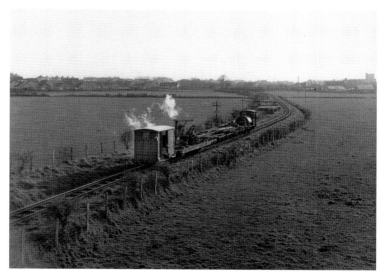

The TR has a series of Halts, usually marked only by nameboard and where a track crosses the line, and they are named after local farms whose occupants they used to serve. Hendy is the first such location east of Tywyn. In 1965, as part of the TR centenary celebrations, the Meirionnydd County Show was held in Tywyn. To ease parking problems a field at Hendy Farm was used as a car park and a shuttle service run to and from Wharf. Here No 2 stands at the specially erected sleeper-built platform. No 1 is at the rear of the train, which comprises the Corris coach and van. The '5' board indicates the start of a permanent way slack.

In 1996 No 1, with a special vintage working, passes the Halt, whose nameboard had recently been vandalised. The roof of the farm building is only a skeleton, and a new sheeted building has appeared behind. *DJM/TE*

Rhydyronen

No 1 pauses at Rhydyronen in the winter of 1941 with its train of one coach and two wagons of slate. The overflow from the injector suggests difficulties with the aged Giffard injectors. The tatty state of the siding point is clear; the siding was used in 1951 to reverse the inaugural Society trains, and later removed.

In January 1956 a new point is about to be inserted into the track, to form a double-ended siding that was, however, never used as a passing loop. Two ex-Penrhyn coaches are being used to transport the gang.

By 1996 the siding has again been removed to enable the curve to be eased and the platform lengthened. No 1 pauses with a vintage special; the south-side look-out on the van was removed during the 1940s. *W. A. Camwell, DJM collection/J. C. W. Halliday/TE*

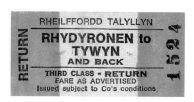

Issued in 1982.

John Adams's classic picture of No 2 and train at Rhydyronen in 1951. The slate-built shelter is typical of the intermediate stations, built when the line was completed and slate readily available. The nameboard was put up by the TRPS.

Forty-five years later the scene is similar. The building has been re-roofed and the track re-aligned to ease the curve. The pipe drains the trackbed. Locos no longer carry a link on the front hook, screw couplings now being used. *J. H. L. Adams, TR collection/TE*

On 21 September 1956 No 4 comes down the bank into Rhydyronen station, past Plas Coch, the home of Hugh Jones and his two sons, Herbert and Dai, all working for the railway. Herbert is driving No 4 and the TRPS President, the Earl of Northesk, firing.

Forty years later Drivers Roy Smith and Mike Davies prepare to stop at Rhydyronen with No 3, bringing a train of air-braked stock past Plas Coch on a driver-training special to improve familiarity with the air-brakes. The gable end of the cottages in Rhydyronen can be seen in both views, but the rest of the area is now much tidier, and the track relaid on jarrah sleepers. *J. J. Davis, courtesy HMRS/DJM*

On one of the two downgrades on the up journey, No 4 passes Tynllwyn Farm with a mixed rake of stock in the 1960s. The TR van and two Brown Marshall coaches head a train with a Glyn Valley coach, a couple of unroofed opens, and the 'cardboard' carriages, TR bogie coaches 9 and 10 which were built on mine car chassis with bodies built at Pendre using hardboard. Two caravans are in the farm field, both belonging to TRPS members. Mrs Jones-Evans provided accommodation at the farm for the Yorkshire Area working parties, and here one of the authors learned the art of dividing oval pies into seven equal portions, under the scrutiny of six hungry pairs of eyes.

In 1996 the trees hide the field full of caravans, and the iron fence has gone. Driven by TR Chairman Winston McCanna, No 3, with a very standardised train, observes the 5 mph limit over the newly relaid track. *J. H. L. Adams, E. Castellan collection/TE*

Brynglas

Loco No 5 stands on the loop at Brynglas on a works train consisting of ex-FR wagons and the chassis of coach 10, which was waiting for a new body to replace the hardboard one; the TR van brings up the rear. The train will be propelled up the line to collect old rail after relaying. There is no block post, only the open frame.

Today an engineering siding has been laid on the right (note the locked bar across the siding to prevent vehicles being pushed out). The loop is now a straight run for the main line, and the points are controlled from the blockpost, the roof of which is visible above the second coach; the point rodding is visible to the left of No 3 as it passes on a train of modern stock. *Both DJM*

No 4 passes through the loop in 1958 with a special train, comprising the two restored Glyn Valley coaches and the two TR bogie 'cardboard' coaches, 9 and 10. Stooks of hay are drying in the field and Pandy Farm is above the line.

Forty years later No 3 and a train of TR standard coaches stand at the same spot; the leading coach is a rebuild of the closed bogie coach (No 9) in the earlier picture. The hedge has gone, following a flash flood in 1993, a retaining wall has been built, and the field has been re-seeded. *J. H. L. Adams, E. Castellan collection/DJM*

This page The first No 7 stands at Brynglas crossing with a Penrhyn open and one of the ex-Corris Railway coal wagons on 31 July 1954. The signal is one of a couple erected by Charlie Uren, but quickly removed as the Railway Inspectorate did not approve of non-interlocked signals.

By 1965 a ground frame has been installed, but the operator has no shelter. Manual staffs are in use, exchanged between the train crews.

Today the block post controls the layout, although there are still no signals and the blockmen use flags to call trains into the loop. No 3 waits while the fireman is in the block post changing the electric key tokens for the single line. A ballast tamper stands on the engineering siding, to the right of the rail stack. *J. J. Davis, courtesy HMRS/ B. J. Ashworth, TRPS Collection/ DJM*

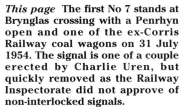

Opposite page Despite the headboard, No 4 has stopped at Brynglas on a special working in 1958; the train contains both Glyn Valley coaches, and the Giesl ejector has not yet been fitted to the loco. Bill Faulkner, for many years a Director of the TR and a regular driver, leans from the cab. Note the crude poles for the telephone line.

In 1996 No 1 stands at the same place. In the background can be seen the block post containing the ground frame and token instruments. The telephone poles have gone, the cable now being underground. *J. H. L. Adams, E. Castellan collection/TE*

No 2 leaves Brynglas with a steam works train on 2 May 1981. The station building is in the trees, and the slate farm shed blends well with the scene.

In 1996 No 1 leaves with a photographic special. The station and farm sheds on the right remain, but a modern metal-clad sheep shed hides much of the train. The 'U' board indicates that the block post, which is visible on the extreme left, is unmanned. *DJM/TE*

It is March 1954, probably Easter, and a working party heads up the line to go ballasting. This cutting was prone to flooding and became known as 'Tadpole Cutting'. No 4 pulls three wagons, and ex-Penrhyn No 8 is well-filled with 'workers'. The track has been relaid, but seems to lack levelling and crowing on the curves. Hugh Jones, foreman platelayer and driver, steps back on to the track to continue fettling it.

No 3 passes the same spot with an up passenger train, and heads into the now well-drained cutting. Brynglas bridge is in the background of both photographs. *R. K. Walton/DJM*

Dolgoch

This page Taken by Bert Chappell on 24 September 1955 'near Dolgoch', the first picture shows No 3 on a down train hurrying along on the patched track. Even Dai Jones, who was the driver, has not been able to identify the exact location, but it is believed to be about a quarter of a mile west of Dolgoch where there is a slight hollow to the south of the line.

In the second picture, taken in the spring of 1941, No 2 poses in Dolgoch woods with a train of one coach, the van and a couple of wagons. Arthur Camwell and his colleagues were the only passengers and the crew were quite happy to stop for photographs. The track joint in front of the loco looks rough. The rails by the van are spares, not a siding.

In March 1996 No 1 poses in the woods with a similar train. The undergrowth is clearer, the track much better, but the tree to the right of the engine is the same oak as seen in the 1941 view. *H. D. Chappell, P. B. Bold collection/W. A. Camwell, DJM collection/TE*

Opposite page Pre-Society views of Dolgoch Viaduct from the ravine are rare, and this view from the north is probably the earliest known view of the TR. No 1 is shown cabless, with only a weather-board, and the van, curiously marshalled at the up end of the train, still has an open balcony.

The main difference today is the growth of trees that fill the ravine, making photography possible only in winter. The viaduct is largely as built, although the spandrel walls were rebuilt in 1970. The footpath is more heavily used these days, and the stream less overgrown. No 3 crosses with an up train. *National Library of Wales/DJM*

No 2 poses on the viaduct in the spring of 1941, with Hugh Jones peering round the chimney.

Forty-five years later his grandson, David, does the same as No 1 stands at the same spot. Not much else has changed. The oak trees are thicker, the track is better and now has stone ballast, permitting the viaduct to drain properly; rails that have been replaced await a gang to come and collect them. A telephone wire is attached to the handrail. *W. A. Camwell, DJM collection/TE*

Traffic was heavy when Henry Casserley travelled on the TR in August 1948, and the train capacity was increased by using four slate wagons. The van was out of use, with defective wheels, so there is only a dubious brake on the engine to stop the train. Without a van, the manager, Edward Thomas, supervises the train from the 1st Class compartment.

In 1996 it is no longer permissible to carry passengers in unsprung and unbraked wagons, so this picture is posed. The scene has not changed greatly, although the platform is now properly surfaced, the track much improved, and the boscage cut back. *H. C. Casserley, courtesy R. M. Casserley (2)/TE*

In the 1920s (*left*) No 1 waits at Dolgoch, with all four passenger coaches. The head of the right-hand rail is breaking away, an ongoing problem with the wrought iron rails.

In the winter of 1941 (*below left*) the train comprises one coach only, plus some empty wagons. The rhododendrons have grown, and the seat has acquired a backrest. No 1 now has the welded saddle tank.

In the 1990s (*above*) the platform has been lengthened and widened, and hard-surfaced. No 1 takes water at the old column with a similar train, including the Museum wagons behind the engine. *TR Collection/W. A. Camwell, DJM collection/TE*

Below A new column was built further east in 1961, when the platform was lengthened, allowing longer trains to be run. The view of the two columns is today hidden by trees, but in 1967 No 4 stands at the new column with the morning train, conveying the tea-van. *DJM*

Right Plan of Dolgoch station, showing the Viaduct. *C. K. Theobald*

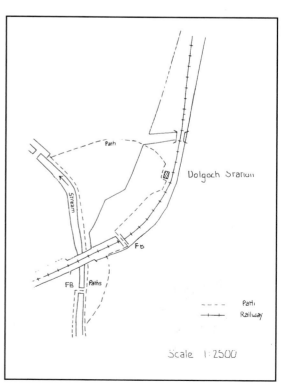

Dolgoch Station

Path

Stream

Fb

FB   Paths

- - - - Path
-+-+-+- Railway

Scale 1:2500

Quarry Siding

This page Quarry Siding Halt is located where a farm track crosses the line near the shale quarry that the TR used for ballast. In the first view No 1 heads a lengthy train of three bogie and six four-wheeled coaches over the crossing in August 1967.

During the winter of 1968/69 a loop was installed at Quarry to enable the railway to run three train sets in the peak season. On a snowy Saturday No 5 and a works train pause at Quarry en route to Abergynolwyn.The formation for the loop has been cleared and crossing timbers lie on the ground for use in the west end points. The siding to the quarry can be seen in the distance. The rebuilt van No 6 is on the train, and the earlier body can be seen beyond the siding as a hut.

In 1996 No 1 heads a vintage train out of the loop, with van 6 at the rear. The siding (on the right) has been re-aligned parallel to the running line and extended westward, mainly for the storage of engineering wagons. *J. J. Davis, courtesy HMRS/DJM/TE*

Opposite page In April 1957 the Yorkshire Area gang has paused from digging ballast to photograph No 3, then working bunker-first uphill. The Halt nameboard is visible above the leading carriage. One of the opens is an ex-Penrhyn coach, the other built at Tywyn.

The same photograph is difficult to take today, as the top of the quarry face is overgrown and unsafe, but the view is little changed from this second one taken in 1969 showing the loop points and Nos 3 and 6 leaving on a two-coach train. The locos are being run in after winter overhauls. *J. C. W. Halliday/DJM*

Above and left No 3 pauses at Quarry Siding with a down train in April 1957. One of the quarry gang rests on his shovel, while others talk to the train crew - maybe lunch is being delivered. Just visible in the trees is No 4 on a rake of wagons in the siding, which look to be full; after No 3 has left, No 4 will go out on to the line to spread the 'ballast'.

Today erosion of the hillside above the quarry makes it impossible to stand in the same spot, and the 'present' view of No 3 pulling out of the loop is slightly higher and further west. The white board is used to help the train crews sight the blockman's flags. The plantation of trees hides much of the valley, but the farm above No 3 in the 1957 picture is visible above the steam in the 'present' shot. *J. C. W. Halliday/DJM*

Below left No 4 on a works train at Quarry Siding. Wagons are being manually shunted on the right, while the slate wagon on the left has been lined to enable it to hold ballast or coal. *Llew Bedder*

Below Digging shale ballast in the quarry at Easter 1959. The bonnet of loco No 5 is visible bottom right. Shale loosened further up the face was pushed down and shovelled on to the conveyor, which fed a hopper over the track and in theory allowed the wagons to be loaded through a trap in the bottom. However, the shale was rather sticky and when left tended to solidify, so the hopper was not very successful, and a walkway was built over the track so that shale could be tipped from wheelbarrows. Disused for many years, since improved finances have allowed the TR to purchase crushed stone ballast, the quarry is now tree-grown. *J. C. W. Halliday*

Nos 4 and 6 shunt a works train into the siding in the spring of 1969. The formation has been cleared for the loop and various materials are on site.

No 3 passes the same spot with a Tywyn-bound train. The loop is in place, and the siding now comes off the loop, but the slate fencing remains. The block post is on the left. *Both DJM*

Between Quarry Siding and Abergynolwyn the line crosses a small valley with a stream and waterfalls, the line being carried on an embankment. At Easter 1967 Nos 6 and 4 double-head the morning train. The tea-van, No 7, heads a mixed rake, including the four TR coaches, the Corris coach, No 18, a Glyn and a bogie brake. On the road a caravanner heads home-ward up the valley.

By 1996 the track is much better ballasted, as No 3 heads an early season train. The leading coach is 21, which has recently had its east end converted to a saloon, primar-ily to carry disabled passengers, but also popular with the general public. The road has been widened, and the farmer at Tan-y-Coed has built new sheds and an extension to the house. *DJM/TE*

Abergynolwyn

Opposite page In September 1953 No 4 approaches Abergynolwyn station with the 3.12 pm from Tywyn. The loco still has its Corris Railway buffing gear, which must have made for a jerky ride, as the coaches were effectively loose-coupled to the engine. The track is still original TR.

Heavy overgrowth means that it is difficult to identify this location today, but the slight cutting through which the train is passing is the same as that shown in the 1996 picture of No 1. The boscage has been cleared and the track renewed, although a remnant of the slate fencing remains on the right. The post at the rear of the train carries a telephone point to enable train crews to contact Control with a plug-in phone carried on the train. *J. J. Davis, courtesy HMRS/TE*

This page On 1 June 1932 No 2 waits at a deserted Abergynolwyn station. The wooden building, dating from the opening of the line, is looking very dilapidated. The siding is visible in the foreground.

In August 1948 traffic required all four coaches and four slate wagons. The building has been replaced by a slate building of the same open-fronted design as elsewhere. The rebuilding is reputed to have been paid for by the Government and the building used as a blockpost during the Second World War; the holes in the end wall were probably for the Home Guard to defend the building from attack up the line. Henry Casserley is photographed sitting in the wagon.

In 1996 the building has been replaced again and an awning added. The platform has been widened and only one track passes in front of the building, the loop having been moved westward, behind the photographer. *H. C. Casserley, courtesy R. M. Casserley/ R. M. Casserley/TE*

Views of trains on arrival at Abergynolwyn have been one of the most photographed scenes on the TR. In 1936 No 2 stands alongside the original wooden building; the piles of slate are for its successor.

In June 1951 the same engine runs round while a group of military look on; the officer seems to be giving orders. The new building is already acquiring a sag in the roof.

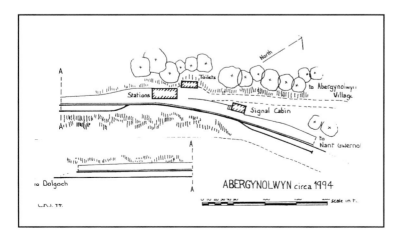

Map of Abergynolwyn station circa 1994. *C. K. Theobald*

62

In September 1967 the shelter was demolished, and the siding for the tea-van removed, so that a proper building, with refreshment room and booking office, could be built. An awning around the new building protects passengers from the rain, and electricity has arrived.

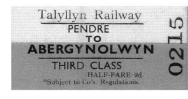

By 1996 the track has been singled in front of the station, and the platform widened and extended eastwards. The points are operated from the block post, and colour light signals control movements. The 'U' on the signal post tells the driver the block post is unmanned and the signals inoperative. The building has acquired a burglar alarm, a sign of the times. *H. B. Tours, DJM collection/J. J. Davis, HMRS collection/DJM (2)/TE*

This page No 1 stands on the extension beyond the east loop points, having propelled the coach and van from the platform to couple on to slate wagons. The line is on a slate retaining wall above the road to the village. The point levers were weighted to be set for one road and had to be held over for the other direction.

In the winter of 1975/76 the station is being remodelled for the opening to Nant Gwernol. The hollow to the right of No 1 has been filled, and the track slewed south, as a platform is being built on the site of the original track. The block post is nearing completion, and the track will be laid in new materials before opening.

By 1996 the platform is fenced and surfaced and a siding has been laid in. The point rodding leads westward to the loop. No 1 waits to change staffs before proceeding to Tywyn. *W. A. Camwell, DJM collection/DJM (2)*

Opposite page No 6 stands at Abergynolwyn in the mid-1950s with the TR van and the two 'cardboard' carriages. The siding used to be on the left where the photographer is standing. The loop has been lengthened and relaid since the TRPS took over, although the ballast looks sparse.

Forty years later the building has been replaced, and the platform widened. The original loop was too close to the rock face to permit two passenger trains to pass, so it has been moved to the west, and the platform extended. No 3 is standing at the station. *TR Collection/TE*

Opposite page Some of the rock excavated during the rebuilding of the extension was tipped at the west end of Abergynolwyn, to provide a wider area for the new loop and western extension of the platform. A temporary siding was laid, carried on timbers, for the tipping. In the distance No 8 stands at Abergynolwyn station.

In the 'present' shot No 3 runs down the new loop where the elevated siding once stood; the tree, top right, locates the site. The colour light signal controlling the loop is in front of the engine. *Both DJM*

This page No 2 runs round at Abergynolwyn on 13 September 1950; the rails are barely visible among the grass. The loop is behind the loco, and the rails in the foreground have been lifted from the siding, possibly to patch the running line, although this is unlikely as Sir Haydn is dead and the railway will close in a few weeks time, its future uncertain.

On 22 May 1976 the rebuilt No 2 passes the same spot with the special train for the opening of the Nant Gwernol extension. Phil Guest, the fireman, is now one of the Locomotive Inspectors. The loop has been moved westward and a long platform, to accommodate two trains, built on made-up ground. The train comprises the modern bogie stock, built at Pendre. *R. K. Cope, courtesy R. S. Carpenter/DJM*

Below right The programme of events marking the ceremonial opening to Nant Gwernol.

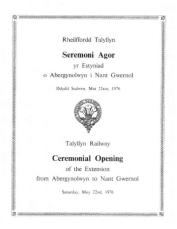

Rheilffordd Talyllyn

Seremoni Agor

yr Estyniad

o Abergynolwyn i Nant Gwernol

Ddydd Sadwrn, Mai 22ain, 1976

Talyllyn Railway

Ceremonial Opening

of the Extension

from Abergynolwyn to Nant Gwernol

Saturday, May 22nd, 1976

This page East of Abergynolwyn the line crosses an access road into Forestry Commission land. In the early 1950s the first No 5 is propelling a train to Nant Gwernol to collect rail from the Alltwyllt Incline. A group of people clusters round the wagon at the front of the train, which may well be off the track. Forestry Crossing is just beyond the train. The lack of alignment in the rail joint in the foreground is very evident!

Forty-four years later No 3 passes the same location with the down 'Quarryman'. Again, the crossing is visible behind the train. The picture is taken from the trackside, rather than from between the rails, for obvious reasons. *Llew Bedder/DJM*

Opposite page On the day after the extension opened to passengers No 1 heads a down train over Forestry Crossing. The crossing was originally protected only by a 'Stop' board, but due to poor visibility and an increased volume of traffic - timber lorries and visitors' cars - this is no longer adequate, and flashing lights have been installed. Today, as No 3 heads down the valley, there is additionally a 'sleeping policeman' designed to slow the speed of traffic. *Both DJM*

This page Halfway along the extension, at Ty Dwr, a stream cascaded down the hillside and under the line. By means of a wooden trough on two slate pillars, water was diverted to fill locos; the trough would be pushed into the stream to start the flow, then a second moveable trough was used to direct the flow into the loco tank. In 1948 No 2 has left its train at Abergynolwyn and come up the otherwise disused extension to take water and be oiled. The driver is Hugh Jones, and the fireman his youthful son.

In 1996 No 1 stands at the same spot. All traces of the columns and trough have gone, and the track was lowered to level out the gradient when the line was rebuilt in the **1970s.** *R. M. Casserley/H. C. Casserley, courtesy R. M. Casserley/TE*

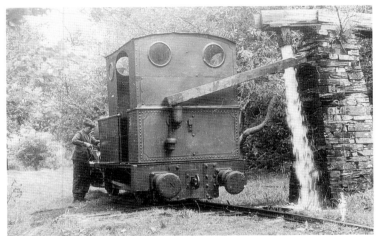

Opposite page At milepost 7, along the extension between Ty Dwr and the winding house, 'Rickety Bridge' crossed a cattle creep and rivulet. In 1967 the beams were rotting and a wagon has been pushed up the line with some second-hand sleepers to patch the track to enable a works train to reach the winding house in order to demolish it. Two very heavy pieces of rail were put in over the bridge to relieve the load.

The bridge was replaced by a culvert and bank when the extension was rebuilt. No 3 passes the same spot; the electricity pole to the left of the wagon can be seen to the right of the loco. *Both DJM*

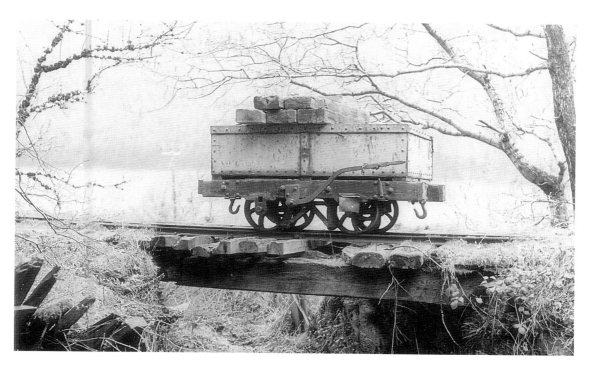

The curve to the west of the winding house gives a fine view over the village of Abergynolwyn. Eric Rimmer's 1967 view was used on a calendar with the title 'The Sylvan Way', and typifies the extension as it lay undisturbed before the line was extended in the 1970s. The rails were there in the long grass, and the track provided a pleasant walk.

Today the view is as good and the slate fencing remains, but the track is neat and tidy. Abergynolwyn Church is below the line at this point, and the name 'Amen Corner' was given to this location by the 'Gwerns' - as the volunteers styled themselves - when they were rebuilding the line, and some of the blasting caused rock to fall on the church roof. 'Amen Corner' was also the name of a pop group of the 1960s. *E. Rimmer/DJM*

The winding house, which held the cable drum for the Abergynolwyn Village incline, straddled the mineral extension; the running line passed through the building, and the incline is down to the left. In 1965 a gang carries out some track clearance.

Today all trace of the building has gone, having been demolished in 1968, and the track is aligned further to the right and raised about 18 inches to ease the gradient. The remains of the cable drum are to the left of No 4; it is to be restored and mounted on a display at the site. *Both DJM*

Viewed from the east in 1966, a wagon is visible through the winding house building. Access to the incline was via a loop round the back (left) of the building, which incorporated a turntable. The track to the incline then crossed the running line in the centre of the building, dividing into two tracks before descending the incline down to the right. The drum axle is in the top opening, and the decayed state of the beam holding up the end wall is clear.

In 1996 No 4 passes the site. The circular casting in the foreground is the housing for the turntable. *Both DJM*

The winding house viewed from the west (downhill) side, showing the cables running down the incline. *J. J. Davis, courtesy HMRS*

74

Viewed from the top of the incline, the roof of the winding house has been removed and the drum is clearly visible. There were two cables, wound in opposite directions to enable wagons to ascend and descend simultaneously, the weight of the descending wagons hauling the others up. The mechanism on the right is the brake for controlling the speed, and the pulleys to guide the cables are visible under the beams. The curved rail at the top of the incline is hidden in the grass.

The Winding House was demolished in 1968, some of the slate being used in the rebuilding of Abergynolwyn station, although its quality was generally poor. Today little remains, but the drum still lies at the top of the incline. *Both DJM*

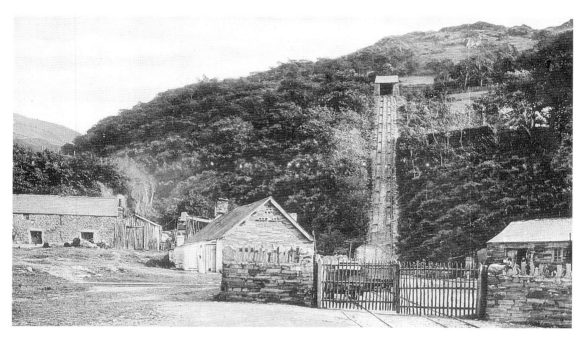

The double-tracked Village incline descended from the extension and crossed the Gwernol at its foot to a small walled goods yard; one of the closed vans can be seen here standing in the yard. The building on the right was a writing slate factory, and the water wheel drove a sawmill. The tracks continued behind the photographer and ran between the rows of quarrymen's cottages. Coal is reputed to have been delivered directly to the domestic coal stores, and the night soil collected by wagon, to be taken up the incline and tipped along the trackside.

Today all the tracks and all trace of the yard have gone, and the incline is tree-grown and not visible at a distance. The building to the left of the yard is still there, although now a house, and the building on the right, behind the toilets, is built on the walls of the slate mill. The incline formation rises above the white estate car.
Commercial postcard, Derek Allen collection/DJM

Nant Gwernol

The approach to Nant Gwernol during the reconstruction. Blasting has started at Big Bend and the 10RB will load the rock into tippers, much of it being tipped at Abergynolwyn.

Eventually the corner is cut away, but the track still remains on the original alignment. In the background the station building is being erected.

Today the permanent track on the new alignment leads into the completed station, where No 4 is running round its train. Some of the temporary track used to rebuild the extension remains in the undergrowth on the left. *All DJM*

Talyllyn Railway

Nant Gwernol Project

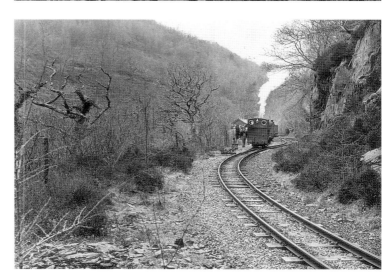

77

In 1941 No 1 shunts a couple of wagons, at least one of which has slate in it. A wrecked wagon lies on the bank behind, probably the victim of a runaway on the incline. The photographer has stood in the same spot as the one who took the picture on page 6 some 40 years earlier.

In 1996 No 1 stands at the same location with two of the Museum slate wagons, one each of the two- and three-bar types; the latter were less numerous. The bluff has been cut back, and the running line is where the centre siding was located. Unfortunately no slate now comes down from Bryn Eglwys Quarry. *W. A. Camwell, DJM collection/TE*

In 1952 the track was recovered from the Alltwyllt incline and the section from Nant Gwernol to the winding house lifted to provide material to patch the main line. The first No 5 is seen here with the recovery train at the foot of the incline. The bent rails from the bottom of the incline can be seen on the right.

In 1996 No 3 has just arrived with the 11.40 from Wharf and stopped at the white board that indicates the fouling point. The alignment of the track on which No 5 stood is now under the platform, and slate fencing protects the drop into the ravine. *Llew Bedder/DJM*

It is the spring of 1976 and Nant Gwernol station is taking shape, although it will be a struggle to finish the line for the opening on 22 May. Mess van 7 stands at the platform, behind the compressor which is providing power to dig out the foot of the Alltwyllt incline to give a little extra length to the headshunt and the loop, on a very restricted site.

Twenty years later No 1 arrives with a vintage special. The platform has been lengthened to provide a path to the footbridge over the Gwernol and the network of forest walks. *DJM/TE*

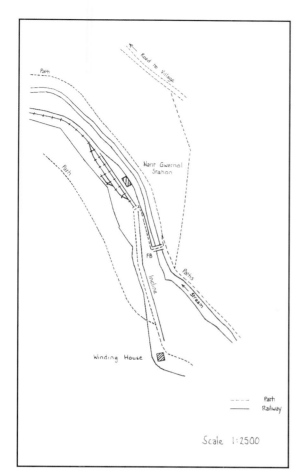

Map of Nant Gwernol station, showing the position of the Alltwyllt incline. *C. K. Theobald*

Looking up the Alltwyllt incline from the site of Nant Gwernol station. Double-tracked, the incline was about 630 feet long, with an average gradient of 1 in 3.5, although it steepened towards the top. The cables ran over the rollers between the tracks, and the winding drum, which perched on a rock ledge above the top of the incline, still remains.

The bottom of the incline has been cut away to lengthen the headshunt, and the incline itself, devoid of track, forms part the forest walks that passengers can undertake in the Gwernol Ravine. The walk continues from the top of the incline along the trackbed of the horse-worked Galltymoelfre tramway, which led to the foot of a second incline, Cantrybedd, taking the tracks to the quarry level. *TR Collection/DJM*

Locomotives and rolling-stock

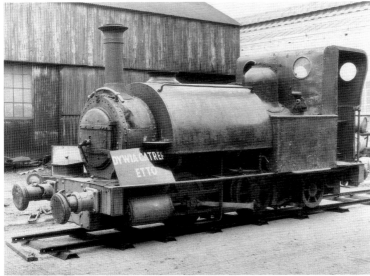

This page No 1 *Talyllyn* stands at Abergynolwyn in about 1900; the driver is probably oiling round. The gadget on the right of the tank is a water lifter, used to extract water from streams and the well at Pendre, probably in dry summers.

The more popular engine, No 1 was out of use by the mid-1940s. It left Tywyn on 24 March 1957 for rebuilding at Gibbons Brothers works at Brierley Hill, where it is seen in the yard on arrival. Much the same as in 1900, the main difference is a welded saddle tank. The sign reads 'I will return home again'.

In 1996, several rebuilds later, the engine stands at Nant Gwernol. The footplate is now more substantial, there are two sand boxes, and nameplates rather than a painted name. Patient work by the engineering staff at Pendre has gradually rectified the design defects in the original loco, and the errors made at the first rebuilding. With boiler pressure upgraded to 160 psi in 1994, *Talyllyn* is now a reliable and powerful engine. *H. C. Casserley collection, courtesy R. M. Casserley/E. Castellan collection/TE*

Opposite page No 2 *Dolgoch* stands at Nant Gwernol in 1941 with Peter Williams on the footplate. Little changed since being built in 1865, the cab is the main addition. The long wheelbase is obvious, the rear axle being behind the firebox, with the valves being driven from the front axle via reversing links - Fletcher's Patent - described as a 'very peculiar motion'.

The rebuilt *Dolgoch* stands outside Pendre shed. Although similar in appearance, little of the original remains. The brass cylinder lubricators above the running-plate are original, but ornamental, a mechanical lubricator now doing the work. The coal capacity has been increased and there are two whistles (the second one since removed). *W. A. Camwell, DJM collection/TE*

Above and above right No 3 *Sir Haydn*, one of three 0-4-0STs built by Hughes of Loughborough in 1878, was rebuilt as an 0-4-2ST in the 1890s and fitted with an enclosed cab. It was rebuilt again in 1920, probably using parts of the other two engines. Seen in 1941 at Aberllefenni, the vacuum pipe has been blanked off after passenger services ceased 10 years earlier. The hinged bar on the bufferbeam was used for the passenger coaches, while the dumb buffers of the wagons rubbed against the beam. Bought by the TRPS in 1951, No 3 worked cab-first uphill as the left-hand side of the cab had no opening due to the vacuum reservoir (see the picture of No 4 on page 86).

Withdrawn in 1958 with a failed boiler, the loco was rebuilt at Pendre with a new one, together with a modified cab to give greater headroom, returning to service in 1969. Seen at Wharf in 1996, the most notable alteration is the recent fitting of an air-pump for the continuous brakes now being fitted on the TR. *W. A. Camwell, DJM collection/TE*

Right The cab on No 3 was very low, as can be seen in comparison to Van 6 behind it in the 'past' picture. During the rebuilding in the mid-1960s the cab was altered to give more height, and shortened so it no longer butted up to the tank. This gave an external coal bunker on the fireman's side, and probably makes the cab cooler as there is less of the firebox/boiler in the cab. On AGM Day 1953, Driver Laurie Earl, of Camden Shed, poses at Abergynolwyn before driving the train to Tywyn. He no doubt felt the difference between the LNWR main line with Stanier 'Pacifics' and No 3 over the decrepit TR track!

In 1995 Driver Jonathan Mann poses at Wharf. The works plates are replicas. *E. D. Bruton/TE*

Built for the Corris Railway in 1921 by Kerr Stuart, No 4 was a standard industrial design, and was out of use with firebox wear when the Corris closed. It was photographed at Corris in 1941. Bought by the TRPS, and generously repaired by the Hunslet Engine Co in the winter of 1951/52, No 4 has been the most-used loco since that time, being reliable and easy to maintain.

Since arriving at Tywyn No 4 has been modified, receiving running plates, stronger coupling and connecting rods, and recently an air-pump. The frames have been lengthened at the rear, giving more room in the cab. In 1958 it was fitted with a Giesl ejector; this made little difference to efficiency and the original chimney was replaced in 1968, the date of the second photograph, taken at Pendre shed.

Named *Edward Thomas* after the former Manager of the TR, the loco has now run for several years as *Peter Sam*, complete with face, masquerading as its twin from the Skarloey Railway created by Rev W. Awdry. *W. A. Camwell, DJM collection/DJM (2)*

THE TALYLLYN RAILWAY COMPANY

THE FIRST "GIESL EJECTOR" FRONT END IN GREAT BRITAIN

The increasing traffic in the 1960s and the poor performance at that time of No 1 led the TR to look for a new loco. The combination of the track gauge, tight loading gauge and raised platforms made it unlikely that a 'ready-made' loco would be found, and after toying with the ideas of articulated locos and of having a new one built, the TR bought a 3-foot-gauge 0-4-0 Barclay tank in 1968. Built in 1948 for the Irish Turf Board (Bord na Mona), and intended to burn turf, it was one of three locos that had done very little work. The boiler, wheels, cylinders and motion would be used to build a new loco. John Bate, the Chief Engineer, designed a neat 0-4-2 side tank, and the loco was entirely built at Pendre over the next 20 years. Named *Tom Rolt* after the founder of the TRPS, it entered service in 1991. The pictures show the Bord na Mona loco on arrival at Tywyn in 1969, and as No 7 at Abergynolwyn for the naming ceremony by Mrs Sonia Rolt. *E. Castellan collection/Murray Dods*

The first No 5 was built by David Curwen using the engine and gearbox from Tom Rolt's famous narrow-boat *Cressy*. Delivered to Tywyn in September 1952, this picture was taken immediately after it had been unloaded, as it made its first moves on the TR. Tom Rolt is on board, and the car behind it on the right is Tom's Alvis. No 5 was underpowered and had a short life, the transmission in particular not being up to railway duties.

The present No 5, a Ruston & Hornsby diesel, stands in a similar position, with the toilet block and station extension altering the background. *Llew Bedder/DJM*

The second internal-combustion-engined loco was a 4-2-0 based on a Mercury yard tractor. It entered service in 1954 and gave reasonable service until superseded by No 5, which arrived in March 1957. Lack of a reversing gearbox meant that it had to be turned on a jack at the end of each journey. Here it stands at Pendre with the motor trolley bringing up the rear.

In 1996 No 5 stands at the same spot, again with the trolley, which now has a roof, at the rear. The barn has been replaced by the carriage shed, and the cylindrical water tank replaced by a larger square tank. The vehicle in the siding is used for transporting the 10RB digger and other large items. *J. J. Davis, courtesy HMRS/TE*

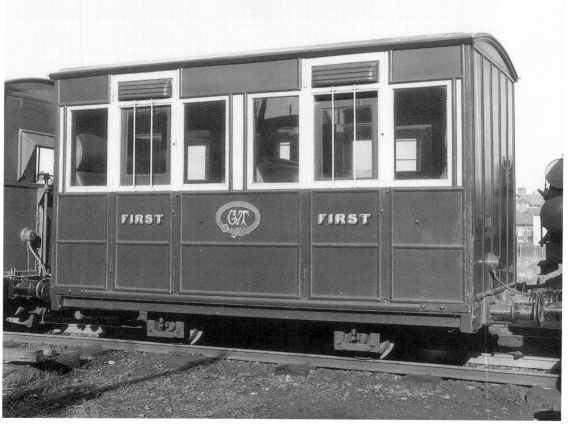

Opposite page The need for more coaches led the TRPS to purchase the bodies of two Glyn Valley Tramway coaches. Two-compartment four-wheelers, they had been sold when the GVT closed in 1935. The 3rd Class coach, built by the Midland Railway Carriage & Wagon Co in 1901, was sold to a farm near Glyn Ceiriog, the former passenger terminus of the GVT. In early 1958 it was moved by TRPS members to Hunt's of Oldbury for restoration; members are seen here pushing the dilapidated body up planks on to a wagon. The other body, located at Chirk Vicarage, was the sole GVT 1st Class carriage.

On the TR both GVT coaches have been restored as 1st Class vehicles, in GVT livery. Ex-Ffestiniog running gear was used and the vehicles have TR side buffers. The lamp housing on the roof is omitted as it would foul the TR loading gauge. As on all TR coaches, the doors are on the north side only. *Llew Bedder/DJM*

This page The 'Stanton Carriage', a 3-foot-gauge coach built by Kerr Stuart and used on a reservoir construction railway, was bought in 1957 from Boden's Stone Ltd at Stanton-in-the-Peak, Derbyshire. It was found to be in poor condition and the balcony body was scrapped. After modifications to the frame and bogies, it was fitted with a five-compartment open body. One and later two compartments were enclosed to provided a brake and luggage compartment. Withdrawn in 1978, it was fitted with a standard body and re-entered service in 1981. It is shown here as received at Tywyn on the wharf edge, running as a four-compartment/brake in 1967, and as running in 1996 with three compartments and brake/guard's compartment. *P. B. Bold/DJM (2)*

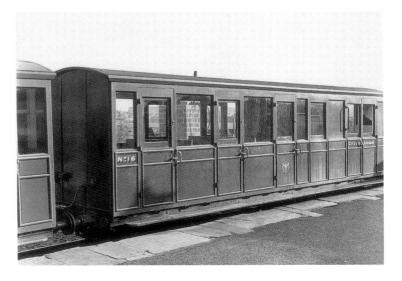

This page With only four coaches, shortage of seats quickly became a problem for the newly formed TRPS. In the winter of 1952/53 the TR was given two three-compartment open coaches that had run on the Penrhyn Quarry Railway. They were coaches H and P, and became TR 7 and 8.

No 7 was fitted with a roof, but was prone to derail, and was little used. The roof was removed and the frame strengthened in 1955, and it then ran satisfactorily until 1961, when it was taken out of service. Rebuilt as the tea-van in 1963, it was used until made redundant by the new Abergynolwyn station in 1969. It was then used as a mess van for the gangs working on the extension. Dismantled in 1980, a new steel frame has been built using the running gear, and fitted with a saloon body, for use by disabled passengers. No 8 ran until 1964 and was replaced by a completely new open coach.

These pictures show No 8 as running in 1954, No 7 running as the tea-van (the upper panels lifted to form a serving hatch), and finally the saloon as currently running. *J. J. Davis/DJM (2)*

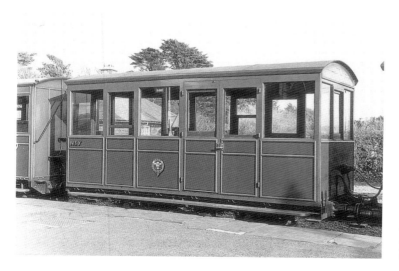

Opposite page Trackwork in Pendre Yard in the early 1950s. The running line and points have been relaid, the latter coming from the Welsh Highland Railway. On the right is an original TR point lever in its cast iron box. A simple facing point lock consists of a pivoted tongue, the hinged end of which drops over a hasp that can be padlocked to keep the point set for the running line.

By comparison the more modern east-end loop points at Brynglas are worked from the lever frame in the block post. A separate stretcher carries the locking bar, with the plunger worked from a locking lever in the frame. The second notch enables the points to be locked for either direction. *P. B. Bold/DJM*

Timetables: 1958, 1964 and 1996

Three timetables illustrating interesting contrasts in the level of services provided, the fares and the general arrangements for passengers and visitors during the Society years.

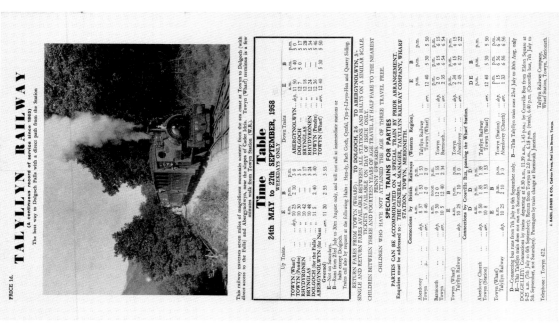

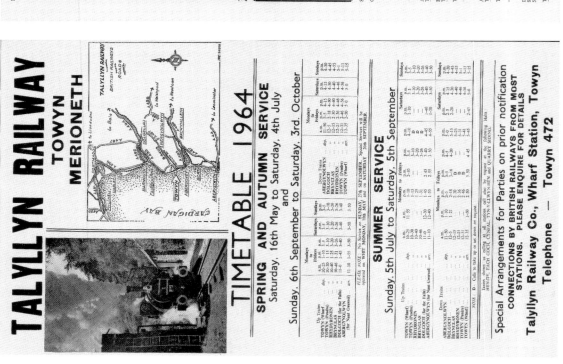

TOCYNNAU · TICKETS

All tickets issued subject to published conditions.

FARES	Single	Return
Tywyn–Dolgoch Falls	£4.50	£6.90
Tywyn–Abergynolwyn	£5.00	£7.30
Tywyn–Nant Gwernol	£5.20	£7.50
Dolgoch Falls–Nant Gwernol	£3.00	£4.20
Abergynolwyn–Nant Gwernol	£1.50	£2.20
Round trip from intermediate stations)	–	£7.50

NEW DAY ROVER BARGAIN FARE Travel all day for £8.50 except for Special Events.

CHILDREN (Aged 5-15 years) Accompanied by an Adult on a full journey return, round trip, or Day Rover £2.00. Unaccompanied, and for all intermediate journeys half adult fare. Under 5 travel FREE

SENIOR CITIZENS & DISABLED PERSONS Reduced fares available.

DOGS & CYCLES There is a small charge.

REDUCED FARES ARE AVAILABLE FOR PARTIES OF 15 AND OVER.

Tickets are available from the Ticket Offices at Tywyn Wharf and Abergynolwyn stations and from other stations at busy times. Otherwise tickets may be obtained from the Guard on each train.

EIGHT DAY RUNABOUT TICKET

Travel as often as you like during any consecutive eight day period.
Obtainable at Tywyn Wharf only
Adults: £20 Children: £10

The Great Little Trains of Wales

NARROW GAUGE WANDERER TICKET

Tickets are issued at Tywyn Wharf and are valid for unlimited travel on all eight 'Great Little Trains' during any **eight** day period, or any **four** days within an **eight** day period.

AMSERLEN 1996 TIMETABLE

AM · PM · Now - 12 hour clock again!

Spring and Early Summer

March 30 to April 4 — Daily

		W	W					
Tywyn (Wharf)	P R dep.	11.40	2.30					
Rhydyronen	dep.	11.52	2.42					
Dolgoch Falls	P R dep.	12.11	3.01					
Abergynolwyn	P R dep.	12.25	3.15					
Nant Gwernol	P R arr.	12.32	3.22					

February 18 to March 24 — Sunday only

		W	W		Q
Nant Gwernol	P R dep.	12.45	3.35
Abergynolwyn	P R dep.	12.50	3.40
Dolgoch Falls	dep.	1.15	4.05
Rhydyronen	C dep.	1.29	4.19
Tywyn (Wharf)	P R arr.	1.44 / 2.00	4.34 / 4.50

Easter Week / Friday April 5 to Friday April 12 — Daily

				Q				H
Tywyn (Wharf)	P R dep.	10.10	11.40	12.45	2.30	3.35		
Rhydyronen	dep.	10.22	11.52	12.57	2.42	3.47		
Dolgoch Falls	P R dep.	10.41	12.11	1.16	3.03	4.06		
Abergynolwyn	P R dep.	10.58	12.25	1.30	3.15	4.35a		
Nant Gwernol	P R arr.	11.05	12.32	1.37	3.22	4.42		

				Q			H
Nant Gwernol	P R dep.	11.15	12.45	1.50	3.35	4.52	
Abergynolwyn	P R dep.	11.20	12.50	1.55	3.40	4.57	
Dolgoch Falls	dep.	11.35	1.15	2.25	4.05	5.00	
Rhydyronen	C dep.	11.49	1.29	2.39	4.19	5.14	
Tywyn (Wharf)	P R arr.	12.04 / 12.20	1.44 / 2.00	2.54 / 3.10	4.34 / 4.50	5.29 / 5.45	

April 13 to May 24 — Daily

				Q			H
Tywyn (Wharf)	dep.	11.40	12.45	2.30	3.35		
	dep.	11.52	12.50	2.42	3.47		
	dep.	12.11	1.16	3.03	4.06		
	dep.	12.25	1.30	3.15	4.35a		
	arr.	12.32	1.37	3.22	4.42		

			Q			H
	dep.	12.45	1.50	3.35	4.52	
	dep.	12.50	1.55	3.40	4.57	
	dep.	1.15	2.25	4.05	5.00	
	dep.	1.29	2.39	4.19	5.14	
	arr.	1.44 / 2.00	2.54 / 3.10	4.34 / 4.50	5.29 / 5.45	

Spring Holiday Week / Saturday May 25 to Friday May 31 — Daily

As July 13 to August 30

Saturday June 1 to Friday July 12 — Daily

		H		Q			H
	dep.	10.10	11.40	12.45	2.30	3.35	
	dep.	10.22	11.52	12.57	2.42	3.47	
	dep.	10.41	12.11	1.16	3.03	4.06	
	dep.	10.58	12.25	1.30	3.15	4.35a	
	arr.	11.05	12.32	1.37	3.22	4.42	

		H		Q			H
	dep.	11.15	12.45	1.50	3.35	4.52	
	dep.	11.20	12.50	1.55	3.40	4.57	
	dep.	11.35	1.15	2.25	4.05	5.00	
	dep.	11.49	1.29	2.39	4.19	5.14	
	arr.	11.04 / 11.20	1.44 / 2.00	2.39 / 3.10	4.34 / 4.50	5.29 / 5.45	

High Summer and Autumn

Saturday July 13 to Friday August 30 (also Saturday May 25 to Friday May 31) — Monday to Friday

				Q				a	
Tywyn (Wharf)	P R dep.	10.10	10.50	11.40	12.40	1.30	3.20	4.10	
Rhydyronen	dep.	10.22	11.02	11.52	12.52	1.42	3.32	4.22	
Dolgoch Falls	P R dep.	10.41	11.21	12.11	1.11	2.03	3.53	4.43	
Abergynolwyn	P R dep.	10.58	11.35	12.25	1.25	2.15	4.05	5.10a	
Nant Gwernol	P R arr.	11.05	11.42	12.32	1.32	2.22	4.12	5.17	

				Q				a	
Nant Gwernol	P R dep.	11.15	12.00	12.50	1.50	2.40	3.35	4.25	5.27
Abergynolwyn	P R dep.	11.20	12.05	12.55	1.55	2.45	3.40	4.30	5.32
Dolgoch Falls	dep.	11.40	12.40	1.30	2.30	3.20	4.10	5.00	5.35
Rhydyronen	C dep.	11.50	12.50	1.40	2.40	3.30	4.19	5.14	5.49
Tywyn (Wharf)	P R arr.	12.05	1.05	1.55	2.55	3.45	4.35	5.29	6.04
	arr.	12.21	1.21	2.11	3.11	4.01	4.51	5.45	6.20

Saturday & Sunday (except August 17 · Z)

				Q				a	
	dep.	10.10	11.40	12.40	2.30	2.42	4.10		
	dep.	10.22	11.52	12.52	2.42		4.22		
	dep.	10.58	12.25	1.25	3.15		5.10a		
	dep.	11.05	12.32	1.32	3.22		5.17		

				Q				a	
	dep.	11.15	12.50	1.50	2.40	3.35	4.25	5.27	
	dep.	11.20	12.55	1.55	2.45	3.40	4.30	5.32	
	dep.	11.40	1.30	2.30	3.20	4.10	5.00	5.35	
	dep.	11.50	1.40	2.40	3.30	4.19	5.14	5.49	
	arr.	12.05	2.00	2.55	3.45	4.35	5.29	6.04	
	arr.	12.21	2.11	3.11	4.01	4.51	5.45	6.20	

Saturday August 31 to Friday September 27 — Daily

		H		Q			H
	dep.	10.10	11.40	12.45	2.30	3.35	
	dep.	10.22	11.52	12.57	2.42	3.47	
	dep.	10.41	12.11	1.16	3.03	4.06	
	dep.	10.58	12.25	1.30	3.15	4.35a	
	arr.	11.05	12.32	1.37	3.22	4.42	

		H		Q			H
	dep.	11.15	12.45	1.50	3.35	4.52	
	dep.	11.20	12.50	1.55	3.40	4.57	
	dep.	11.35	1.15	2.25	4.05	5.00	
	dep.	11.49	1.29	2.39	4.19	5.14	
	arr.	12.04 / 12.20	1.44 / 2.00	2.54 / 3.10	4.34 / 4.50	5.29 / 5.45	

Sept 28 to Nov 2 — Daily

				Q	
	dep.	11.40	12.45	2.30	3.35
	dep.	11.52	12.50	2.42	3.47
	dep.	12.11	1.16	3.03	4.06
	dep.	12.25	1.30	3.15	3.15
	arr.	12.32	1.37	3.22	3.22

			Q		
	dep.	12.45	1.50	3.35
	dep.	12.50	1.55	3.40
	dep.	1.15	2.25	4.05
	dep.	1.29	2.39	4.19
	arr.	1.44 / 2.00	2.54 / 3.10	4.34 / 4.50

Please Check Notes

a Arrive 15 minutes earlier
C Calls on request only
P Car Park available
Q 'The Quarryman' - runs daily March 30 to November 2
R Light Refreshments available
W In the event of extreme weather, please confirm that trains are running
Z A special service will apply on August 17

British Rail Station 300 yds.

RHEILFFORDD TALYLLYN

Rheilffordd gul yw Rheilffordd Talyllyn syn defnyddio injans stêm ar pob un o'i threnau cludo teithwyr. Agorwyd hi yn 1865 ac maen rhedeg o Dywyn sydd ar arfordir Bae Ceredigion i Nant Gwernol. Gorwedd llawer o'r lein ym Mharc Cenedlaethol Eryri gyda rhaeadr ewynnol yn Nolgoch a rhodfeydd

Arbedwyd y rheilffordd rhag cau yn 1951 gan Gymdeithas Gadw Talyllyn - y gymdeithas gadw gyntaf yn y byd. Cefnogir y rheilffordd heddiw gan aelodau'r gymdeithas gadw syn gweithio ar y trenau a chynnal y gorsafoedd. Mae'r aelodau yn cynnal a chadw'r rheilffordd o ddydd i ddydd gyda llawer o weithgareddau eraill. Gellir cael mwy o fanylion am aelodaeth y gymdeithas gadw drwy gysylltu â ni.

DISABLED PASSENGERS

There are disabled toilet facilities at Tywyn Wharf and Abergynolwyn stations and a special coach is available for wheelchairs except on "Heritage" trains. It helps to let us know that you are coming.

SUNDAY NIGHT OUT BY TRAIN

14 July - 25 August
Train leaves Tywyn at 7.00 for entertainment at Abergynolwyn, arriving back at 9.55. Special fares.

	Sunday evening
	7.00
	7.12
	7.31
	7.45
	7.52

	Sunday evening
	8.00
	8.05
	9.05
	9.21
	9.38
	9.56

Additional trains will run on Sundays May 26 and August 25 and during the Autumn School Half-Term holiday.

All trains call at Tywyn (Pendre), Rhydyronen and Brynglas by request/
See poster on stations.

NADOLIG · CHRISTMAS

SANTA SPECIALS

These will operate on Saturday and Sunday 21 and 22 December at 11.00 and 2.00.
Advance booking is helpful.

CHRISTMAS TRAIN SERVICE

Trains will depart Tywyn at 11.40 and 2.20, daily from December 26, 1996 to January 1, 1997, both dates inclusive. Please inquire for full details.

INDEX